How to trade the markets

I0444138

The various books on trading tend to be very optimistic and promise great profits if you follow a particular formula.

I don't believe that such a magic recipe exists.Its been my observation through years of trading in a variety of markets that every person is unique.

In that sense you can't teach anyone how to make money in a particular market.You must in my view find your own individual path.

That of course is easier said than done.

I hope through this book I give you the tools to at least point you in the right direction.

Chapter 1

In my view you must find yourself before you can actually trade and make money.You may not have the personality to trade.

Perhaps you don't handle risk well.Maybe you simply can not absorb the pressure of risking your cash.

To even consider the concept of trading a particular financial market you have to make a journey into yourself to understand if you are willing to go on a highwire without a net.

When you formulate a plan on how you wish to execute a trade there will be no one ready to catch you if you fall.

I suppose you are curious why I don't simply give a group of illustrations on how to make a quick buck in a particular market.

I think that would be a mistake. First you have to really look at yourself and ask a simple question. Am I ready ?

Can I survive if I lose in a big way ? What is my breaking point ? Let's face it, markets are fascinating but they can be cruel.

When things go well you can feel invincible. But when every trade is a failure it can feel devastating. If you're not mentally strong it can really hurt.

So before you're ready to start trading you must have an honest conversation with yourself. You can Bullshit everyone. But you must be honest with yourself.

The fact is if you are not ready to take a risk the odds are you will not succeed.

Chapter 2

I first began trading during the 1987 crash. My Dad had urged me to invest in the stock market. But I was reluctant since I had limited knowledge in the markets and was nervous about taking any risks.

After a great deal of discussion I finally listened to my Dad. My first investment was very boring I bought the phone company.

Which at that time was basically a monopoly. When I purchased the shares for 32 ⅝ I was concerned about the health of the stock market.

My worries included the fact that based on following the market it seemed over valued.But to me the market always seemed over valued.

I purchased the shares on thursday a few days before the crash and quickly got so nervous that I sold the shares for a ⅜ loss.

I was in Florida at the time and called my Dad in New York.I told him I was scared and sold the shares for a loss.He yelled at me in Yiddish that I did not have any blood and hung up on me.

I quickly called him back but he would not talk to me.My Mom and Dad were both Holocaust survivors.

They were a bit neurotic but in a good way.My Dad was a redhead and usually acted like a redhead.

So his temper was very predictable.Suffice to say the market dropped a hundred points on friday and my telephone shares were below the price I sold them.

Of course I had no idea what would occur in a few days.But every instinct I had was telling me that the market did not feel healthy.

The traditional measures of the stock market were overvalued but that in itself has never interfered in a bull market.

Needless to say the market dropped almost 22 percent on Monday and my telephone stock dropped to 24 ¼ to my total surprise.

Even this old and very conservative investment took a huge plunge.I quickly called the electronic trading dept at Manufacturers Hanover Trust.You could not get a live broker so I used the system that allowed you to trade on a phone without any human involvement.

In 1987 it was a unique way of trading.

So with very little experience I placed a market order for the same stock I sold for more than 8 points higher a few days ago.

I filled at 24 ¼ which was a surprise since my order should have filled higher and within an hour the stock was trading over 29.

I of course rushed to sell and pocketed a 5 point profit in about 1 hour. That was the beginning of a turbulent trading experience which made me lose my 50 percent profits of that week in the following 3 months.

Of course I never stopped trading and after all these years I am still addicted.

Chapter 3

Since I have traded for many years I often have individuals ask me to teach them how to trade. I tell them that trading is more an art than a science.

You can learn many of the elements of trading such as technical analysis or fundamental analysis. But that in itself will not guarantee that you will be successful.

That is because you have a great deal of competition. Everyone else has access to the same information you do.

If you know the technical elements of a particular stock or any other market you can be sure many other people do as well.

The same is true for fundamental analysis. The point is you need to have either unique knowledge or a different approach to how you trade the market.

The most valuable tool is your own feel for the market. So how do you teach that ? In reality you can't teach a mysterious element like intuition.

But you can learn how to size up the market and make a series of quick assumptions. In my view you can use all the tools available to you but if you don't have luck then you are less likely to succeed.

The best traders are smart and have skill but their success has also involved luck. Some believe that the most successful people create their own opportunities.

That can also be true in trading but with more nuisance. You can develop your own recipe for a successful trade but first you are going to have to do some work.

My advice is simple. You must read and read and read as much as you can. Knowledge is power and there is no easy way to gain information.

You must use the library or online resources and gain as much knowledge as you can on all aspects that involve the markets.

That means reading the New York Times and the Wall Street Journal. You can get a short term subscription to the Financial Times as well.

You must learn the basics of Technical analysis and as much command of Fundamental analysis that you can.

Yes I know this is hard, it takes work. But this is only the beginning.

Chapter 4

For me to illustrate the importance of knowledge is ironic. The majority of people who have traded in recent years know very little about the particular stock or investment they have made.

They tend to follow the momentum and make money when a bull market is filled with greed and lust.

The desire for funny money is intense and as others are making a quick buck the greed only intensifies.

In my experience the more quick bucks you make the more you will eventually lose. Making money trading currencies or bonds or commodities and of course stocks is hard.

You need to be prepared. You have to study the particular investment you want to make. Its irrelevant if it's for a few minutes or 30 years.

If you just follow the crowd you will eventually lose your shirt. Its just a matter of time. I realize I sound old fashioned.

But experience has taught me that if something is too easy then there is always a price to be paid. In short periods of time you may win but the markets will draw you in. And that is when probability will eventually get you.

You have to be very strong to walk away with your chips. Very few people have that ability. With the amazing bull markets in recent years it's easy to feel invincible.

But the reality is the more powerful the up move the more intense the eventual down move.

So why am I even talking about this ? Because to be a good trader you must be disciplined and you have to control your greed.

If not you will not last long. The mysterious entity we call the market will get you. And teach you a lesson.

This is not speculation it is the law of nature. So if you love to gamble you should close this book right now.

You will hurt yourself by trading the markets. Whatever you make you will lose in a short period of time.

The urge to trade is powerful but sometimes the smartest thing to do is nothing. That is right. For me doing nothing is hard but often it is the best approach.

So many opposite forces could be moving a particular market that it is hard to determine which side of the trade you should trade.

In the next chapter I will discuss playing both sides of the market. The objective is taking advantage of the volatility.

Chapter 5

I realize it sounds counterintuitive. How can you play both sides of a trade at the same time ? It sounds ridiculous.

I know. But there is logic to this approach. Especially when you are taking advantage of Vol. When you have a high Beta event. A situation where a market can make a big move.

It could be the Consumer Price Index or an important earnings announcement or a variety of events that can be responsible for a major move in a particular market.

That is when your gain will offset your loss. I have used the NVDA earnings statement as such an event.

Of course you have to make sure you are not overpaying for whatever you are buying. That is not always so easy.

That is why you have to watch a particular market before you buy. You need to be familiar with a particular asset class before you use this strategy.

I would use options to gain leverage. So for example if NVDA were trading at 870 before the earnings announcement. I would purchase lets say 3 Calls and 3 Puts with a Strike Price of 870.

When you buy at the current price of the stock it is called In the Money. So when the stock moves up or down you get more bang for your buck.

In a recent release NVDA made a 15 percent move up. My Puts fell hard but of course my call rose in value.

When my loss for the Puts were offset by my gain I started to look for an exit strategy. In my example I spent about 15000 USD for the Call and 15000 USD for the Put.

When I closed the trade. My profit on the Call was about 39000 USD so after deducting about 13000 USD for my loss on the Puts you could say I had a nice profit.

The key to this trade was to not pay a premium on the options. My technique is not to buy right before the news event.

At that time interest was at its peak so buyers of those options already made them expensive. So when do you buy ?

That is the hard part. The only way you have a chance of not overpaying is watching the trading pattern of the contract.

That means getting a feel for how it trades under different circumstances. I know it sounds strange. But the more you watch a particular event the more likely you will notice a pattern.

This is something that you will be used to after you study a particular stock or a specific market. Everything has a pattern. Including you and me.

We have our habits and actions that are predictable. Well even markets develop a pattern over time.

It's those actions that can give you an edge. You can make a great deal of money if you are lucky enough to find that pattern in a particular market.

Chapter 6

The classic example in my trading since I began after the 1987 crash is Gold. It will sound amazing but I made large amounts of money simply trading Gold between 280 to 290.

I leveraged my position by buying large amounts of Gold stocks that were trading below 10 USD a share and often below 3 USD a share.

When I detected a pattern in the price of Gold I began to watch the Gold stocks. I also was looking for a predictable economic environment with interest rates relatively stable.

Gold settled into a boring trading pattern. It found buyers around 280 and sellers started to take profits as the metal reached 290.

On its face it sounds like a real yawn. So how do you make money if the asset you are trading is making a very small percentage move over a month or two.

That is where leverage comes in. If I bought Placer Dome a Canadian Gold mining company with substantial Gold holdings.

I could make healthy profits by entering the trading range at 280 and selling near 290. If I bought the stock at 3 USD and had 50000 shares.

I could make a great profit by just playing the spread. So a ⅛ gain was a nice profit and of course a ¼ gain was even better.

I had a few years where I made millions of Dollars by just watching the boring movement in Gold and playing the spread on a Gold stock.

If I was confident that a firm had low Volatility then I was willing to take a large position. When I was doing this type of trading.

Placer Dome was considered one of the top Gold mining companies. So It was not a great risk for me to take a large position. There are no guarantees in anything. But if you prepare for a trade by studying the stock and the industry. You will have an advantage that could increase your probability of success.

The most important element is increasing your probability of making money. Things can happen that can throw off your careful plans.

That is why you should not follow the crowd. They can be right for a short time but eventually they will be very wrong.

Chapter 7

I have had many occasions where people ask me how they can start trading. I tell them that they must read as much as they can.

Knowledge is power.And it is more true when you trade then almost any place else.The mysterious entity we call the market is an instant voting machine.

Of course this machine often goes to extremes, that is the moment that a good trader can take advantage.

This happens all the time.The conglomeration of people we call the market get emotional.They are too bullish or too bearish or simply indifferent.

These situations all offer opportunities.You simply have to detach yourself from the masses and learn to think in a rational manner.

This is easier said than done.Some of us are not wired for pressure or pain.The market can definitely supply a lot of that.

You have to look into yourself and ask a simple question.Can I handle the pressure ? Can losses drive me crazy or can I wait it out.

Only you know.If you don't have the personality to be a trader you should stay away.Whatever money you might make is not worth the aggravation.

Believe me I have been on both sides of the street.When I had a Hedge fund I was miserable when I was losing other people money.

I felt I betrayed the people who trusted me.Of course I was simply a victim of market conditions but emotionally I felt awful that my positions were losing me a great deal of money.

You are the only one who knows what you can handle.Its easy to have fun when you're making money but trust me when things are not going your way it hurts yeah in a big way.

So in explaining to you how to be a trader I am also illustrating how to not be a trader.Perhaps you really don't know.

Well I guess experience is the best teacher.When you eventually fall on your face that will be your first test.

At that point you will know if the wonderful world of trading is for you.

Chapter 8

As difficult as trading can be it is even more difficult to decide if the trading environment is correct.

Too many people play the markets without watching the relationship of what they are trading to other markets.

For example if you were doing fast trades with NVDA you probably didn't care that the dollar was falling in Europe.

Or that the price of Iron ore was dropping sharply in China.These issues matter and can have a bearing if your particular trade is successful or not.

If Iron ore is dropping in China it could indicate a slowdown in the economy.If that trend continues then the market for NVDA and its chips could drop in the country.

My point is that you can't simply trade a particular stock or bond and not pay attention to other markets.

You certainly could make money for a certain amount of time but eventually reality will affect your trade.

This is the most difficult element in being a successful trader. The popular form of trading in recent years is to follow the herd.

Who cares what the stock does ? Why bother doing research ? The masses are pouring into a particular investment and everyone's making money.

That is a recipe for disaster. Yup I sound like I am trying to spoil the party. But the truth is that is the reality.

It's hard to trade and even harder to make money. An understanding of the markets is crucial. And a reasonable understanding on how different markets affect each other is even more important.

Trust me I get it. The power of making a quick buck is magnetic but everything has a price. If you make a fast buck it eventually will make you have quick losses.

That is simply how it works your luck will run out and then you are hooked. Of course you want to make it back.

And if market conditions suck well guys you will be in a world of hurt. That is why preparation is the key.

Not only do you have to prepare yourself for the possibility of losing money and perhaps your entire investment.

But you have to study and learn as much as you can to understand the world around you. I have discussed the relationship of other markets to your particular trade.

I have not even mentioned the situation all over the world. Is there a war brewing or is it a current threat to your particular trade.

Yeah I know so many things to think about. Well dudes welcome to my world.

Chapter 9

As I am writing this I find it ironic that I am implying that to be a successful trader you need a great deal of knowledge.

But the truth is you need a great deal of knowledge to be successful in anything.The difference is the lack of knowledge can impact your trade almost the second you place it with your broker.

It is not as hard as it sounds.I suggest you read the New York Times and the Wall Street Journal every day.

You not only will be better informed but you will be more equal with traders who are professionals.

To be successful in anything requires work.So why should trading be any different ? After you begin reading more about current conditions I suggest you use the Web to learn more about an area of investments that you are interested in.

Perhaps you are fascinated with the Oil market or 10 year Treasury bonds.It really does not matter.

I have found a way to make money in almost every market.There is always a trend or a trading range.

Also assets get over priced and under priced.In other words humans are emotional and that characteristic shows up in markets.

Now it could be argued that Computer programs remove emotion from the equation and the Large Language models could at some point completely take over markets.

After all, if a method is developed that is smarter and faster than humans it certainly will be used more by various financial institutions.

But frankly a good trader can and will in the future learn the weaknesses of any AI program. In my view since humans are imperfect then anything they design or create will be inherently imperfect.

Nothing is without flaws, it's just a matter of finding it. My point is simple you never know what small amount of knowledge could help you when you're making a quick decision.

I have often made a fast trade or quickly reversed my position because somewhere in my little brain I had an insight.

If you asked me what it was I could not tell you. But somewhere in some isolated neuron was a microscopic amount of data that gave me an opportunity to have a successful trade.

In other words trading is an art not a science.

Chapter 10

So how do you formulate your next flirtation with the market ? It's great to talk about trading but what is the process ?

How do you decide what market to trade or what your next trade will be specifically ? Well that is as individual as your fingerprints.

You have interests and you have an area of the market that fascinates you. The first thing you need to do is take your potential trade for a test drive.

Now your particular trade could be time sensitive. If it is the results of a drug trial or a FDA decision on a particular therapy.

You will have only one opportunity for executing that trade. So lets be more general. Lets say you believe Gold is about to pop so you decide to watch NEM.

It's the largest Gold miner and it has its own characteristics. It has a distinct pattern when the market is going up or down.

It moves differently when interest rates are moving up or down. It changes direction based on the value of the dollar.

It could be accumulated when war is being threatened in the Middle East. It moves in accordance with current Central bank policy.

It may rise or fall based on demand in India or China. As you can see there are a variety of reasons a particular investment may go up and down.

These factors must be put into any scenario you may have when deciding if or when you want to make a trade.

It sounds complicated because it is. Yeah it's a lot different than buying the current hot stock on Social media.

It's not as exciting as riding the current wave among day traders. And it does not appear to be as much fun as just chasing the current momentum stock.

The difference is my method is boring but will work over time. How do I know ? Because when you have traded long enough you have seen everything.

The current hot investment, the euphoria, the greed and of course the crash of the hot investment that can do no wrong.

Yup that trade worked great until it didn't. Nothing changes only the people change. But the factors always stay the same over time.

I hate to say it but boring works far better over time. You don't need my book or any book if you simply want to follow the crowd.

The problem is the crowd is always wrong……..eventually.

Chapter 11

Let me illustrate to you the stranger aspects of trading. I had bought my Parents a house in upstate New York.

I took them to a shopping center in Newburgh and did what everyone else would do. I took a walk. The market was open and I had a few ideas in my little brain that I was considering.

Sometimes ideas bounce around in your head and you don't even know it. At the time I was gambling on takeovers.

I use the word gambling because that is exactly what it is, gambling.

When a stock is in play, meaning the big boys are speculating on a possible acquisition the moves could be huge.

You could go to the bathroom and come back and have a stock moving on large volume that is up or down 30 percent.

I have seen these spikes many times. It's fun when you're on the right side of the trade but of course you can be on the wrong side as well.

I had passed a pet store and something lit up inside me. I had been considering an investment in a food company that had takeover rumors for 2 years.

The symbol for the company was PET.

Nothing had happened so I decided it's just rumors.But suddenly I had an interest and just walking past a pet store had ignited some mysterious force in my trading personality.

This was the early days of cell phones.I had the first phones since my Mom and Dad insisted that I call them every day.

But I left the phone at the house since I was with my Parents and most people did not have a cell phone.

So I went to a pay phone and dialed the 800 number to the brokerage firm.In those days you could do a trade on a touch phone so I quickly made a large trade on the food company.

I not only placed a block trade but decided to buy more.I don't know why I was so aggressive but something was pushing me to make the trade.

At first the stock was as exciting as watching grass grow.But in 3 months I made a lot of money.When I woke up early one morning there was an announcement that a large food company was buying the firm.

This was just a few days after I called Investor relations and asked probing questions to the manager of the department.

It was obvious to me that the guy was hiding something.But somehow I had the sense that a takeover was coming.

I apparently was not imagining it.So in a strange twist of events I made a major bet on a takeover that actually worked.

Can I explain the process ? No way but who cares.It was a great trade.

Chapter 12

I don't mean to imply that deciding on your next trade will come out of the air.And I am not recommending that you develop dubious methods to formulate your next trade.

I simply want to illustrate that the business that is known as trading has mysterious features.If you analyze my actions that day.

You could easily say it was pure luck.Why I decided to make a large trade or the mechanics of the investment is not important.

The results were the only important factor.But I think that is the wrong approach.As I mentioned earlier all the facts and data we accumulate can be useful at some point in the future.

I am an advocate of reading and reading and reading.You dont know what data point may be useful to you someday.

If you have knowledge you have the tools that can be handy at some point in your future.As I see it the combined knowledge and experience I had accumulated somehow came together that day in a shopping center in Newburgh.

If I had not studied the company and not watched its personality as a trading vehicle I never would have had the confidence to place a large trade.

On some type of unconscious level I had been considering a speculative trade on the stock.It did not come out of nowhere.

At the time food related takeovers were becoming popular again.These cycles happen often on Wall street.

That in itself is a riddle wrapped in a mystery inside an enigma. We are often a mystery even to ourselves so sometimes our trading pattern could be a surprise to ourselves and the people we love.

I hesitated to even mention this story since I am usually very analytical when deciding on my next trade.

But we are human and sometimes do things that even we do not understand. I suppose in that case I was lucky since my Dad would often tell me that I had more luck than brains.

He was kidding of course but he did believe that luck was the most important factor in any success.

As I have gotten older I have seen that my Father was absolutely right. The greatest success stories in our civilization have involved luck.

Yes you can make your own luck. But at some point the element of serendipity is always a factor. I am getting off track here.

Rather than waiting for some magic moment I suggest that you look into yourself and find what interests you.

At that point I believe you need to be a hunter. Study your prey, watch its behavior and when you believe the time is right you strike.

Believe me if you watch the movements of a particular stock in a certain industry. You will find patterns.

What do you think a sophisticated Computer program does ? It does it more quickly and more efficiently than we do.

But the premise is the same. Once you notice a pattern then you will develop a formula for making money when that stock makes a particular move.

I know it sounds hard.But trust me it can become second nature.In time it will become very easy.The more time you put into this effort the more simple it will become.

I suspect that the mysterious trade I made in Newburgh was based on years of study and many hours spent analyzing the food industry.

The trade was ready. I simply had to carry it out.

Chapter 13

How do you eliminate bad habits ? It's ironic but any flaws you have will affect your ability to trade successfully.

I tend to stick to a particular trade for too long.Eventually that investment will go against you.The longer you trade a particular stock or industry the more likely it will stop working.

But how do you move on if a particular investment has been successful for you ? I realize that no matter what I say here the average trader will only change their approach when the investment starts to lose money.

It's human nature we believe we can change course quickly and will have the ability to start fresh with a different approach.

In my experience that is easier said than done.So the question must be asked why even mention it ?

Because if you stay too long in a particular trade it could turn ugly sometimes very ugly.Let me give you an example of one of my big failures.

I had developed a groove in trading stocks that were related to the Coal industry.There were years that the market was tanking and my trades were making me big money.

In fact some years I made as much cash as my trades in Gold.Of course that was true until it was not true.

The leaders in the industry had often said that they were in a super cycle.So not only were the coal related firms doing well as coal prices kept rising.

But there was enormous speculation that a particular company would be involved in a takeover.So the industry was bubbling on all cylinders.

Commodities have a history of being a contrarian investment to the Stock market.That is nothing new to Hedge funds or money managers.

But what is also true is that the executives in their own industries are often too close to the action.What is clear to outsiders is rarely noticed by those in the inside.

That was a huge mistake.Not only for the leaders in the industry but to traders like myself.When things started to turn I was stubborn.

I averaged down and averaged down and averaged down.Yes I brought my cost down but it didn't matter because eventually every major coal company went Chapter 11.

The executives who paid a large premium to acquire coal assets were holding investments that went to zero.

In that scenario it was impossible to make money unless you were short.I was fooled by all the talk of a super cycle.

I could not imagine that all the largest coal companies had to go out of business and start fresh as they formulated a new game plan.

The fact that they came back as new companies and took advantage of the new bull market in coal did not help the investors in their firms before they went out of business.

Chapter 14

Why am I talking about this ? The fact is everyone makes bad trades just as everyone screws up.

How often do you come across people who always talk about their success rather than the fact that they have made mistakes in their life.

It's part of growing and becoming a better person.Its important to discuss this since you can not become a good trader without having the characteristics that can make you successful.

It's crucial that you not have a big ego or turn into an arrogant prick because you made money and are suddenly feeling invincible.

If that happens then it will be only a matter of time before you fall on your face.And trust me that sudden reality will hurt.

Oh yeah it will hurt big time.

So how do you become a better person with the personality to make you a successful individual ?

I guess this is a question that has been asked by much smarter people than me since the beginning of civilization.

I suppose the easy answer is to look into yourself. Yes look at a mirror and accept your weaknesses and try to improve yourself any way you can.

I discuss this because your weaknesses will appear when things go badly for you. And believe me that period in the cycle will occur.

I have often said that if I have 51 or 52 percent successful trades during a particular period of time then I am doing great.

After all Wall street is the biggest casino. So why should trading in the greatest casino be any different.

It's amazing but 90 percent of my trades have been successful. But that figure is deceptive. Some of those losing trades like the coal trade have been huge failures.

So the percentage does not tell the whole story. I think the key to my success is not being stubborn as I was with the coal trade.

No matter how successful you are over time in many ways you are your worst enemy. My weakness my stubbornness is what made the coal trade not just a failure but perhaps the worst trade I have ever made.

Needless to say I have analyzed that point in time many many times. I of course have never averaged down on a losing trade to the extent I did then.

But market conditions are always the key factor as to how large your failures can be. And that is something that no one can predict.

Chapter 15

I am giving a variety of ideas I have had in the years I have been trading.But I have been reluctant to discuss the most important factor in my success.

That mysterious element is intuition.I ask myself how can I teach the average person to have a feel for the market or anything close to it ?

In reality you cant.Its something that you possess or dont.Its like teaching someone to be sensitive or aggressive.
In my view although you can't teach intuition you can illustrate how that characteristic can develop.

For example if you begin to recognize the relationship between other markets that skill can begin to give you a feel for many of the markets.

This is learned through trial and error.For example at this time in May 2024 the stock market is worried about inflation.

But the reality is the market does not care what the inflationary outlook is at any given time.It goes up every day regardless what the latest news is.

Today the PPI was higher than expected.The market had a minor drop and then rallied on a revision of the index from a previous month.

As I am writing the market is up even though the more important CPI is coming out tomorrow.So what is the market telling us ?

First off the market does what it feels like doing and no amount of news will change the direction of the trend established by the majority.

But what if the market is wrong ? Can you just follow the masses off a cliff or what ? This is the hardest part of trading.

Your own opinion is often a hindrance to your success.I can tell how many times I have been right about a particular news event or Government economic statistic.

The problem was that I was right but the market decided to go in the opposite direction.So I either stayed out of the market since I thought the PPI would be higher than the consensus but the market went up anyway.

In my years of trading this has been the most difficult element to have successful trades.After all we all have opinions about countless situations.

But the market opinion is the only one that counts.Now its true that this mysterious entity we call the market is often wrong.

The market gets too bullish and too bearish.But the majority of the time following the direction of the market will make you more money then trading based on your opinion.

In other words it doesn't matter if you are right or wrong it does matter what the market is telling you.If it is bullish regardless of the news.

You better pay attention or very soon there will be a hole in your pocket.And sometimes it will be a very big hole.

Chapter 16

At this point I have been giving you some ideas that I have about trading.But the truth is you shouldn't copy me or any trader.

You need to gain knowledge and you should test your ideas in simulated trades.You could start with small amounts of money.

Or with as much cash as you are willing to lose.Hey losing is part of the game.And I did not use the word game as a random event.

Let's face it the world of trading is a game and as I have said the greatest casino in the world.You know it is funny when I walk into a Casino in Las Vegas it all seems so small to me.

The fact is it is small, especially when you compare it to Wall street.

After you complete your simulated trades you then should read the newspapers.My Favorite is the New York Times and the Wall Street journal.

Also the Financial times could give you a sophisticated outlook of the business world from a British perspective.

You will gather this data and you will form a consensus in your mind.Yes you will I know….. for people who have not paid much attention to the financial world this seems like Science Fiction.

But trust me as you read more and pay more attention to various markets you will form opinions.Of course you could be completely wrong.

But that is how you will learn.In other words dont be afraid to fail.The more bumps and bruises you obtain from trading the better you will eventually be.

The concept of trial and error is so true when you are a trader.I have learned that every day is different.

So if you had a bad day.You will just forget about it and you will start off fresh the next day.With some luck you might wash away your losses from the previous day.

It can happen you simply have to develop thick skin. That is easier said than done but trust me if I can do it you will gain that ability as well.

As you can see I am a big believer in doing. The talking part is easy. The way to learn anything is to do it.

So as you are reading this book, start reading and learn more about our planet. The more you learn every single day the more prepared you will be to battle the various markets.

And make no mistake about it you will be in a battle. Not only with the market but with yourself.

Chapter 17

So let's use an example. I sometimes could study a stock or an industry for weeks before I decide to take the plunge.

I might decide the Oil market looks interesting. For simplicity sake I will not discuss trading the commodity directly.

Although there is always an ETF that is available for you to trade almost anything. But we are mostly discussing stocks so we will keep the discussion on oil companies.

Suppose BP had a recent earnings report that disappointed the street. The stock has found support at the 50 day moving average.

That is around 43. It is trading with the rest of the group which is following the price of the commodity since OPEC voted to lower production.

The economy in China is getting weaker and the demand in Europe has dropped because the war in Ukraine has suddenly heated up.

The shale oil drillers in America have been lowering production since the price of oil is too low to make a good profit.

New tension is growing between Israel and Iran and the price of oil is reflecting the tension.Nervous traders are bidding up the price on any rumor.

So now you can see the different factors that could affect the future success of my trade.Oh one more thing BP is going Ex Dividend in 5 days.

I mention this fact for a few reasons.First the big oil firms usually pay a fat dividend.If you buy prior to the Div you could ride the wave of investors who want to capture the payout.

This lowers your risk on the trade.Sometimes if you wait for the Div you could lose money on the trade but the payout makes it a successful trade.

But timing is everything.If you buy a day or so before the Div you may overpay for the stock.Deciding when or if you should play that game is a judgment call.

I have to make it a factor because I like to buy a stock when its going Ex Div in a short time.Especially if the market sucks.

If you're playing defense a Div is a great way of increasing your odds of making money on the trade.

I decide that the tension is so high in the gulf that any factor including the activity involving ships entering and leaving the area could set off a rally.

So the factors have aligned.BP is trading at the low point of its range and is holding the 50 day moving average.

The yummy Div is coming up soon and the trigger happy traders on the NYMEX are ready to give oil a nice ride.

So I make the trade and watch the different factors that could help me make money on the trade.This is an actual trade I have made.

The price of crude was basically dead and I lost a small amount of money on the trade.But the Div gave me a profit after all the factors were included.

As you can see a great deal of factors can affect the probability of a particular trade being successful.

Ironically in a boring market the old reliable Div could be the deciding factor on if you make money or not.

It's hard to make money every day so you use any factor to gain an edge.If it has to be a Div then more power to you.

Chapter 18

It's said that you learn by example so let me give you another example.The CRSP stocks are not popular when I am considering a trade on CRSP.

The company had an FDA approval on its therapy for a difficult condition that affects people of color.

The therapy is very expensive and requires approval of private insurance firms and the insurance programs managed by various governments.

The market is lowering the valuations of CRSP and other stocks in the same industry.CRSP had a recent earnings report which basically said nothing.

Sometimes the news cycle is boring.But companies have to say something to the street and to investors.

CRSP is drifting toward 50 far below its 52 week high of 90.The market is near all time highs as recent inflation data indicated that recent increases in inflation are slowing down.

As a result interest rates had dropped about 50 basis points.But was pointing in the opposite direction as the Federal Reserve was still not ready to lower rates.

Investors were optimistic but were getting impatient.So do I wait for the market to digest its recent gains ? Do I take advantage of weakness in the CRSP stocks ?

Do I buy the stock or use options for the transaction ? Owning the stock gives you more time if the trade goes against you.

While options require less cash and can give you more leverage.If I buy options how much time do I want ?

The longer the time period for the option the higher the cost.The higher the cost the higher the stock must go before expiration to make money.

What if the acceptance of the new drug is too slow ? What if insurance firms are not willing to pay for the therapy ?

What if CRSP is forced to discount the cost of the therapy so often that it is losing money on the drug ?

What if patients get serious complications from the treatment ?
What if CRSP is overwhelmed by a new treatment that does not require so much preparation ?

The treatment is revolutionary but requires samples from patients that require processing at specialized facilities.
Do you have a headache yet ? Yeah a trade can be complicated especially if it involves a company with a new drug.

So why even bother, why not just stick with less complicated companies ? Well I don't believe you need to limit yourself.

I think the entire market should be a possibility when deciding on a trade.So What do I do ? I take a position with a one year option.

The market starts to drop and CRSP drops 10 percent.After a further drop I buy more options and lower my cost.

When CRSP reaches a breakeven I decide to exit stage left.I make or lose a few bucks and watch a few weeks later as CRSP moves up 15 percent.

So did I sell too soon ? The market was looking weak.Should I have had more patience ?

Frankly I did not care.Tomorrow is another day.

Chapter 19

Sometimes the best trade is to do nothing.Hey guys it sounds easy but it's hard.Every part of your being wants to do something.

Who cares what.But doing nothing is the hardest thing that a trader can do.Why is it ?

You get used to a certain routine.And trading almost becomes part of your day.You feel like you did not eat that day or you missed an important part of your routine.

But that is a big mistake.If you become an addict.An individual who has to trade.Well you are going to make a lot of bad trades.

This is sort of the zeitgeist of every trader.They have a need to do something.I have found that I have made more money in a particular period when I have decided to stay out of the action.

That word action is a warning sign.It is used by gamblers.You don't want to become a gambler.But believe me that can happen easily.

In fact when my trades become more speculative I know I am running out of ideas.That is when I stop my trading.

It's hard to do.But I realize that it is the healthy approach.Just remember that when a market is dull it usually calls for you to go quiet.

The tendency is to look for something that does not exist.You can't create a good opportunity.If it does not exist then it does not exist.

In time something will come along even if the market is doing nothing.I have tried to create something from nothing.

The trouble is I often would end up with nothing.So just like love it's not a good idea to force it.If it's not there it's not there.

In fact doing nothing has often made me a lot of money.The market would take a plunge and everything I was thinking of buying is suddenly a great deal cheaper.

I can't tell you how many times I pushed myself to make a trade when the market felt expensive. Well in a short time my trade would be down 10 or 20 percent.

I would be angry with my itself. Why didn't I wait ? Why was I in such a hurry ? As a trader you feel you have to do something.

No guys that is a big mistake. You have to learn to be patient. Oh yeah that is easier said than done.

Chapter 20

I can imagine you guys have a lot of questions. So I will try to answer a few here.

How can I just read everything ?

What I mean is learn more and read more. The point of the matter is more that is the main objective.

I have given a few examples but you can't predict the future. I can't use a magic formula to predict the course of your life or mine.

But I can be a wise man in one respect. In my experience every bit of data can become handy in some way.

Not only as a trader but in your life. That is why I say that you should constantly be learning. Your thirst for knowledge should be infinite. So where do I start to be a real trader ?

That is easy. You start by doing. You start by falling on your face. You start by feeling the pain. Yes failure can help you in your desire to not only be a trader but a good trader.

But you have done it already. How can I know that worked for you can work for me ?

Because my concepts are universal.I am talking about knowledge I have discussed the importance of doing.

What can be more universal than that ? To advise someone to constantly expand is not a concept that would work for one individual.

Without knowledge you have no chance in trading or in life.In my view without data we are nothing.Of course you must know how to use that information.

How we do that is our calling card like our fingerprints.You are unique so you will find your path.If you simply try to copy me or anyone else it won't be genuine and it wont work.

So is reading a newspaper everyday part of the equation or just reading anything you feel like doing ?

Keeping informed is a must.I dont believe you can be a good trader over time if you are not connected to the world.

And reading the best newspapers is the best road you can take to stay informed.Its hard enough to analyze the markets.

It's such a mystery how the various markets feed off each other. If you have a decent knowledge of the planet your job will be so much easier.

Chapter 21

The most difficult aspect of trading is understanding the relationship of different markets.The permutations are endless.

The dollar against the bond market the oil trade in conjunction with the stock market. The bond market and how it influences the dollar.

The possibilities are endless. And I have not even talked about politics in America. Or what happens in our world from a day to a week or to a month.

In other words the possibilities of your trade being influenced by what economists call externalities is only limited by your own imagination.

So how do you wrap your arms around such complexity ? Well many people try to ignore it. While others try to use computers to manage the uncertainty.

I mention this aspect of trading because we are experiencing a revolution in AI. The new programs will give tremendous power to the ordinary citizen.

The concept of a Large Language model or LLM is in my view a great opportunity to level the playing field.

That is not to say that there is not great risk. Not only to many industries and to the future of man. But the possibilities are very exciting.

Let's use this discussion in the analysis of various markets and how they relate to each other. As I am writing this I decided to ask Claude this question.

How does the current 10 year treasury bond influence the cost of commodities and the Dow Jones Industrial average ?

The 10-year Treasury bond yield influences commodities and the Dow Jones Industrial Average in several ways:

1. Interest Rate Effect: The 10-year Treasury bond yield is closely watched by market participants as a benchmark for long-term interest rates. When the yield rises, it typically signals higher borrowing costs, which can negatively impact companies and consumers. Higher interest rates make it more expensive for businesses to finance operations, investments, and expansions, potentially slowing economic growth and weighing on stock prices, including the Dow Jones Industrial Average.
2. Opportunity Cost: Higher Treasury yields increase the opportunity cost of holding non-yielding assets like commodities. When yields rise, some investors may shift their funds from commodities to bonds, causing a decrease in demand and potentially lower commodity prices.
3. U.S. Dollar Strength: Rising Treasury yields often attract foreign investment, boosting demand for the U.S. dollar. A stronger dollar makes commodities, which are typically priced in dollars, more expensive for holders of other currencies, potentially reducing global demand and putting downward pressure on commodity prices.
4. Inflation Expectations: The 10-year Treasury yield is also an indicator of future inflation expectations. If the yield rises due to higher expected inflation, it could increase the demand for commodities as a hedge against inflation, potentially driving up commodity prices. However, if the yield rises due to expectations of stronger economic growth, it could have a mixed effect on commodities, as stronger growth could increase demand but also lead to tighter monetary policy, which could be negative for commodity prices.
5. Risk Appetite: Changes in Treasury yields can influence investor risk appetite. Higher yields may encourage investors to shift towards riskier assets like stocks, potentially boosting the Dow Jones Industrial Average. Conversely, lower yields may drive investors towards safer assets like bonds, potentially weighing on stock prices.

It's important to note that the relationship between Treasury yields, commodities, and stocks is complex and can be influenced by various other factors, such as global economic conditions, geopolitical events, and supply-demand dynamics in specific markets.

Not bad for a model that was just introduced to the public in the last year.Imagine this tool is only a baby.Some would say that it is being generous.

So my struggles with the relationship of various markets could be helped by using this new avenue of gaining information.

Will it help you make money ? Perhaps but since everyone else will have access to the same data the game might still stay the same.

The market is an accumulation of opinions which are based on information.The more data which is available the more difficult it is to make a profit.

In a world that has a Large Language model running the show.The probability of large profits are reduced.Because there will be less surprises.

But that does not mean that there are not opportunities.And you can not assume that a mere human can not figure out a way to beat the machines.

If you think the competition between the Russians and the Americans and the Chinese and the Americans is heated.

I now can give you a new competition that will make the Democrats and the Republicans look like a children's game.

The ultimate game of survival.Man against the machine.

Who do you think will win ?

Chapter 22

When I ask the question the average person will always say the machine.But as I have said many times if man has created or designed a machine then its possible that this creature could ultimately beat this entity in more ways than you can calculate.

What does that have to do with trading ? A lot………… because when you trade you are making a variety of assumptions.

I don't want this book to gravitate toward philosophy but these points need to be made.Because of our background we have inherent prejudices.

You and everyone on the planet can have the same facts but we choose to interpret them differently.

That is how we have a market. If we all perceive the world in the same way the difference in price between buyer and seller would be very narrow.

The only entity that would make money would be a computer program. There it is. The machines again. They are always lurking somewhere.

Usually somewhere over your shoulder. As I am writing this computer programs are completing more trades than ever before.

It's happening because humans are making money. So does this lower the probability that you will make money on a particular trade ?

Not necessarily. Because most of these programs make money on the spread. They jump on any opportunity to make a buck no matter how narrow the profit margin.

They can make a huge amount of trades in a short time so we are basically dealing with volume. So how do we mere organic creatures make money ?

Oh yes it's all about the patterns. Even these entities we call machines get lazy and become predictable.

For example the machines like to come into the stock market at the end of the day. Often but not always they amplify the existing zeitgeist of the market.

If the Nasdaq had been in rally mode for the past few hours they might enter the arena by doing more buying of Amazon.

So when I have considered closing a trade I might wait for the last few minutes or seconds to close out my position.

Of course you should never do this on days when options are expiring because the volatility could destroy your trade.

I have learned that the hard way.In fact you should stay out of the market whenever options are expiring.Believe me it is not worth it.

You could get screwed big time.

I am spending a great deal of time on computer programs for a reason.Up to this point they have been a major player.

With AI they will get much bigger.Perhaps they will completely dominate the markets.But either way they can not be ignored.

If you want to be a trader you will have to understand how the machines are influencing the market.

If you dont you will find out the hard way.And trust me it will cost you money.

Chapter 23

Can a machine learn about intuition ? I suppose anything is possible but I doubt it. The concept of having intuition is mysterious so how do you teach it ?

For traders like myself the unknown element of having a feeling is crucial. How many times has the market felt heavy or lacking in energy ? That has happened many times to me and the fact is that feeling is rarely wrong.

It's sort of like explaining the concept of falling in love. Why does it happen ? Can you explain it ?

Good luck with that. In my view there are factors around us that we can not explain. If we don't understand it then how could we add it to a computer program.

Or make that data available to a LLM. The latest iteration has a hunger for information. As it incorporates the latest data into its storage of information it changes.

It becomes a different entity. Certainly different than the original intent of the computer scientists. This new life form is in the process of becoming what it ultimately will become in the future.

A future filled with hope and danger. After all without proper safeguards this new creature could present a threat to humanity.

But in the ultimate bargain it could improve every aspect of our existence. So what does this have to do with trading.

Well everything and nothing. It depends on your perspective. In the short term the computer programs that already have a tremendous effect on the markets will only get more influential.

If you can add a variety of intellectual aspects to the decision that a computer program makes, the entire concept of trading against the machines will become more difficult.

For the purpose of this book we can only assume that these changes will not affect the financial markets in the short term.

The major brokerage companies will do a great deal of testing before they commit large amounts of cash.

So this piece of literature will not be antiquated before it even gets into print. I have felt it necessary to talk about AI because it is that enormous unknown that has to be factored into any trade that will occur in the future.

After all, how many of you guys will want to compete with the machines ? Deep down we believe it is no contest.

Of course I think you are wrong. I firmly believe inferior creatures like humans will always find a way to survive.

I doubt that trading will be any different.

Chapter 24

Earlier in this book I discussed betting on Vol. I gave an example of taking a position on the long side and the short side when NVDA had its earnings report in Feb 2024.

Well now it's May 2024 and NVDA just had its earnings report. So what did I decide to do. I have cited how important it is sometimes to do nothing.

I decided to go long on NVDA even though the risk was much greater than before. Could a Large Language model understand that humans were getting nervous about NVDA and its dominance in the AI universe ?

I suspected as NVDA was trading closer to its latest report that the street was expecting a great deal. As a result I decided to gamble that the Vol would be lower.

When you take both sides of a trade you need sufficient volatility to overwhelm the loss on the other side of your trade.

I made a small profit on my last trade on NVDA because it jumped 15 percent to the upside. This was enough to cover for my losses on the put which I purchased.

This time I was going naked. Meaning I was not covered if NVDA should drop after their earnings report.

So how do you teach that logical reasoning to a Large Language model or any computer program ?

At this point in time you cant. My rationale was that wall street would expect so much from the NVDA report that the division between buyers and sellers would lower the overall move on NVDA.

Well that was the bet I made so how did it work out ? Well guys I got lucky. The earnings were good but not fantastic.

The metrics were enough to keep the stock from dropping which was my fear. Imagine beating on earnings and a larger profit margin than the street anticipated and future revenue above the consensus was still not enough in the first few hours for a big move.

In fact NVDA was only up about 3 percent and dropped below that point as well.

I purchased an ETF that gave about double the movement of the stock. I also bought options on the ETF.

When NVDA only moved up 3 percent after hours I got nervous and took my profits which were about 6 ½ percent.

The stock moved up another 1 percent after I closed the position. The next day when trading had more volume the stock moved up as much as 10 percent.

I still had my option position and sold with about a 90 percent profit. Its was very close to a double.

So what did I learn here ? First off the street gets nervous when the security has already moved up almost 95 percent for the year.

The demands of investors gets higher and higher. Any normal company that had the metrics that NVDA produced would have gone up to the moon.

But NVDA had a weak initial response until the firms following the company raised their price targets for the stock.

Chapter 25

There is a reason I am giving details on this trade. It is an easy way for the reader or listener of this book to get into the mind of a trader.

You might wonder why I was willing to take a position before earnings when I knew that the demands of investors would be so difficult ?

Also with that much risk to the trade why go in naked ? Meaning why not have some insurance ?

Well guys when NVDA released its report about 4:20 Eastern time.I watched as the stock bounced around as analysts were going through the report.

For a few seconds it dropped about 20 points.And I thought to myself why didnt I buy some protection.

But the stock quickly recovered and then rose about 3 percent.The next day when normal trading began the stock was up as much as 10 percent.

But that was not enough movement to compensate for any puts I had purchased at the last earnings report.

I was very nervous that the shorts were just waiting for the report to drive down the price of the stock.

I was fighting with myself that perhaps the results were not relevant.I speculated that maybe some Hedge funds were going short and were not concerned about the details of the report.

My bet was simple.Since we are early in the AI extravaganza that NVDA still had room to go to the upside.

The day will come when the shorts will have a feast but we have not arrived at that point yet.Whoever figures that out will be making a lot of money.

For now let the momentum lead to eventual trading in the sector.NVDA is giving the semiconductors a reason to rally.

They will stop when they feel like it.I doubt that anyone will figure out when that will be.

Chapter 26

Can you be more right than the market ?

It's an interesting question but the answer is always the same.Don't even try.I have tried and the results are often the same.

I dont win.And don't get me wrong I am usually right the trouble is the market usually does not agree with me.

Yeah I could be right a day later or a week later or a month later or a year later.Yup I would be right but I would have a hole in my pocket.

In other words if you have a big ego the market will take care of that. You will get your ass kicked and trust me the pain will be very enlightening.

The mysterious force called the market will put you in your place. You will learn very quickly that anything can happen in a market.

And I mean anything. If you are more willing to listen to what the market is telling you well you will have a fatter bank account.

Hey we all have opinions just remember to not have those ideas interfere with your trading. Its a very difficult experience.

You have to leave your outlook at the door. The only opinion that counts is Mr. market. That entity will determine if your experience as a trader will be fruitful or not.

Trust me dudes it took years for me to control my urges on wall street. It took years for me to be sensitive to wall streets needs.

Whatever success I had up to that point was luck. The street is always giving off signals. It is your job to figure out what all those signals mean.

It then will be your responsibility as to what you do about it. To me it's crucial to absorb this concept.

Everything gives off signals.You are a detective it's your job to study the clues and act on them in a manner that will make you money.

It's not easy in fact it often can be more difficult than you can contemplate.But if you want to reach nirvana in financial terms you will have to learn how to read those signals.

Chapter 27

At this point many of you are asking this question.How can I read these signals ? I am not that knowledgeable about the markets.

This all sounds too hard.Well it is hard but you have to start somewhere.Let me give you an example.

I have cited the strange phenomena of the market reacting to economic news in a way that you would never contemplate.

Yes the good news is bad news scenario or the bad news is good news experience.Let me say that predicting how a large group of people will react to anything is very hard.

When your money is put at risk it is a great deal harder.Because essentially you have to be a psychologist.

I dont have the intention of discouraging you.I simply want to illustrate that the markets can be very difficult to predict.

That is why it is crucial for you to try to get an advantage. Of course what you decide to do must be legal.

When you read about insider trading it's easy to see why this occurs. Not simply to make a buck but because making money on wall street can be very difficult.

People are irrational. They can be very emotional. So the effect on any market can be very difficult to understand.

But there are ways of predicting certain moves by the market. For example if a market is determined to move in a certain direction it will find a way to ignore any news that is counter to their narrative.

In the bull market of 2024 the stock market ignores negative news regarding inflation. But if the economic news is even mildly positive the market decides to rally in a big way.

So if the CPI is due in a few days the stock market may begin to be more defensive. But many times it rallies into the news.

That is typical behavior when the bulls are running on wall street. Of course when fear and pessimism is running hard in the financial district it does not matter what the news is saying.

After a short rally the bulls give up and the existing trend continues. So I guess this is another way of saying that the trend is your friend.

It's very difficult to stop momentum.And it does not matter what the direction is.As I was saying it requires an understanding of human nature.

I suppose understanding man is crucial in every area of life.But in the markets it affects you every time you decide to risk your cash.

Chapter 28

It can be very discouraging when logic is not a key element on wall street.But often it is at those times that you can make a great deal of money when you decide to go against the crowd.

The old joke is you have to be the Maytag repairman.A famous commercial that showed a depressed repairman who had nothing to do because he had the awful job of fixing Maytag appliances.

Well if you have the chutzpah to go against the crowd and you have good timing you can clean up as the followers all lose their cash.

Of course you need luck and a great deal of confidence to go against the crowd.The probability of your trade being a loser is high.

Because you can be so right about the market but so wrong about the timing.Its said that timing is everything and it can't be more true than when you are trading.

So how do you go against the crowd ? You have to go in knowing that on a historical basis you will lose your bet.

I can't tell you how many times I have gone short when I thought the Nasdaq was looking too extended and how many times I have lost my investment.

That is because I would usually use options and time would not be on my side. Even when I have used options that expire in a year or longer I would often have a trade that I would barely break even.

This is often because I paid a high premium for the options and the stock was simply not moving in my favor.

Of course when I have been right the payoff has been huge. I often would be angry with myself that I didn't have a bigger position.

You also have to realize that when I make such a bet the numbers are often in my favor on a historical basis.

For example the VIX is extremely low which indicates the market is too relaxed and is too confident.

I will talk about the VIX in the next chapter.

Chapter 29

To many people the Volatility index is a complete enigma.It is known as the Vix and measures a variety of factors.

But mostly it is a measurement of fear.It makes this conclusion based on the ratio of calls to puts.

The problem is the index has not behaved in a manner that gives traders any clues to the markets next move.

Some experts believe that other measurements are being used by Hedge funds and a variety of traders.So the true value of any moves by the Vix is difficult to determine.

But I think the Volatility index still has value.On a historical basis when the index trades around 12 it is considered an indication of complacency.

The normal range is about 18 and when the index stays at a low level for an extended time it means that a bull market continues to rampage in the area of wall street or a correction is getting close.

In the bull market of 2024 the Vix has been low for a long time.The purchase of protection or puts is much lower than the large volume of calls.

But When the Vix trades at around 12 it is a reason to pay attention.It indicates the market is confident and simply has no fear that the market will lose value in the short term.

Historically that is a recipe for disaster.When everyone is convinced the market can only go up well that is the time to run for the exits.

When you are long in such an environment it is a good time to buy some insurance.It is cheap since very few individuals are buying.

The crowd is doing you a favor.You can trade and have a certain level of protection without paying a large premium.

It's ironic but when the market is booming that is the perfect time to have a certain level of insurance.

Lucky for traders who like to hedge their position it's a great time to have a certain level of insurance.History has taught us when the Vix trades at a low level it usually means the market will in time have a nasty correction.

The question is not if but when.This period will be no different.As of May 2024 it looks like the market will never go down.

Yup many traders have seen that before.Just remember things rarely change in time everything gravitates back to its equilibrium.

Trust me guys this period will be no different.

Chapter 30

To me watching a variety of indicators is something you just have to do.But it is not crucial like watching the numbers on a Plane or a Spacecraft.

Without being dramatic those numbers can save your life or the passengers on your aircraft. With the markets sometimes they work and sometimes they don't.

Let me give you an example. As I am writing this the Sentiment index for Investors Intelligence has a 59 percent bullish rating.

This indicator has been rising as the bull market gathers strength. Traditionally Hedge funds and other large traders would increase their protection.

But that is not happening this time. In fact the opposite. The Vix is asleep while the markets could not be more relaxed.

This is while a war is still going on in Gaza and the Ukraine continues to get pounded by relentless Russian attacks.

This is while China increases its bullying of Taiwan and makes the probability of conflict with the small country even higher.

So what does the stock market do ? What has the Bond market been doing ? How about a big fat zero.

But and this is a big but. The Dollar is still strong even with the probability of lower interest rates in the next few months.

I believe you see the fear in the precious metals. Gold has made new highs and buying continues among Central banks.

Remember when I said the VIX is not the same. Well the action in precious metals could explain the lack of fear in the Fear index.

Markets always adapt, they change their colors, they try to absorb the facts and to act in the most efficient manner.

Well over time not necessarily in the short term. Right now the markets are reaching an important point.

If Government statistics do not cooperate the markets will have to give up some of their gains. This is especially true in the hot stocks like NVDA.

This is not a prediction, it is how markets work. The problem is the adjustment takes time.

Chapter 31

When I said sometimes the smartest trade is doing nothing. I wasn't kidding. It's Also the hardest trade you can make.

Or not make. So many times the Government numbers are confusing. They make adjustments to previous numbers or they just don't seem accurate.

Some people are cynical and believe any Government is going to manipulate the final statistics so why pay attention ?

Well in America the majority trust the agencies that formulate these figures. They are crucial to a market that is reliable and trusted all over the world.

Massive amounts of money flow through the various markets in the U.S. and they depend on accurate and honest results.

I mention this for one simple reason. The markets often do the opposite what you expect and as a result you can make a big mistake if you trade.

Sometimes the stock market will do a complete 180.And you are often mystified and sitting on a big loss.

I said trading is hard and believe me I have the bruises to prove it.So how do you know what to do ?

It all sounds too complicated.I might as well buy a lottery ticket.

Well you can reduce your risk.You can learn to read the market the same way you can connect to someone you love.

It takes time but as you follow the various trends and begin to recognize patterns you will have successful trades.

Some luck could help but after you gain enough experience it will become easier for you.There will reach a point that your research and study will combine with your experience to make you as comfortable as driving your car.

Sometimes I think my body is faster than my brain when I am driving.But a magical thing has occurred.

A part of your brain is so familiar with your car and your senses have become so attuned to how the vehicle relates to the road and its surroundings.

That your driving around a certain area becomes part of your existence.You dont think very much when you go to the bathroom.

Your body pretty much knows what to do.Well the same experience that occurs when you drive your car will in time occur when you trade.

Not all trades but a certain percentage.That of course will be unique to your situation.

The important factor is how much time you are willing to devote to this enterprise.Will this be a hobby or a potential business ?

That will be up to you.And only you will be able to answer that question.

Chapter 32

There is a big difference between the present moment in time and when I began trading.Of course technology has always been a factor.

But today you could say that it is the only factor.OK so I am being dramatic.But the truth is the markets are not wrong about AI.

They always are too optimistic at the beginning of the new thing.The valuations in the stock market at the beginning of the internet were totally crazy.

But investors were not wrong, the web did become everything they expected the details were a little different.

Of course they were a lot different.The same will be true of the Large Language models and whatever replaces them.

I am sure the programs will be much different than what they are today.The scary part is they will be much smarter.

I suspect we will have to find a way of keeping them from working together.And safeguards will have to be created so that the web is not wide open to them.

But the upside is incredible.You name it and that area of our world can improve.Most likely in ways that we can not even contemplate.

But as is true with every technology the downside is very very scary.My job here is to not discuss the effects on society.

But I am discussing AI again because it is the great unknown.How will trading be effected on Tuesday or next week or next month.

Who can even guess what this industry will become in 10 years or 100 years.But what is certain is it will have a profound effect on trading.

But I am also certain that no matter what the programs do they will develop a pattern.And that is when your job will come in.

When all is said and done all your study and your experience in the market will come down to that simple fact.

If you can find a pattern then most likely you will find a way to make money on it.In my view it doesn't matter if it's AI or any other factor.

Good luck, you're gonna need it.

www.ingramcontent.com/pod-product-compliance
Lightning Source LLC
Chambersburg PA
CBHW071220240526
45470CB00018B/2075